Dawn of a new age

MAKING
THE
MOST
OF
YOUR
LATER
YEARS

SUSAN HARDWICK

kevin
mayhew

First published in 2003 by
KEVIN MAYHEW LTD
Buxhall, Stowmarket, Suffolk, IP14 3BW
Email: info@kevinmayhewltd.com

9 8 7 6 5 4 3 2 1 0

ISBN 1 84417 033 0
Catalogue Number 1500571

Cover design by Jonathan Stroulger
Edited by Nick Fawcett
Typesetting by Richard Weaver

Printed and bound in Great Britain

Contents

Acknowledgements

Scripture quotations are taken from *The Message* (copyright © by Eugene H. Peterson, 1993, 1994, 1995, 1996, used by permission of NavPress Publishing Group) and from the Holy Bible, New International Version (copyright © 1973, 1978, 1984 by the International Bible Society, used by permission of Hodder & Stoughton Ltd). The extract from *I Am Collecting Rainbows*, by Father Carlos Valles SJ, was published by Gujarat Sahitya Prakash, Anand, 1985. The final reading in the book, from Revelation 3:19b-4:1a, is taken from the Youth Bible, New Century Version, Anglicised Edition (copyright © 1993 by Nelson World Ltd).

Foreword

Dawn of a New Age suggests that the 60s should be seen as the dawning of a new era or phase of life. It emphasises the huge value and importance of this age group to their communities and to society as a whole, with their wealth of accumulated experience and wisdom.

Many of the daily tasks of getting, rearing, working and building can now be laid aside, allowing this age group to concentrate their energies on those things that they have always wanted to do. This phase of life is also a time for looking back, making peace with situations and events in the past that are burdensome memories and laying them gently aside. It is a time, too, for looking forward and preparing for that last great journey through death, to the Life beyond.

In this book, reflections, prayers, meditations and relevant biblical quotations are drawn together in order to address some of the issues that can preoccupy people, at one time or another, during the later years of their lives.

Susan Hardwick

Introduction: Rainbow people

My heart leaps up when I behold
a rainbow in the sky;
so it was when my life began;
so is it now I am a man;
so be it when I shall grow old,
or let me die!
The Child is father of the Man;
and I could wish my days to be
bound each to each by natural piety.

My heart leaps up when I behold
William Wordsworth, 1807

Students of U3A (the University of the Third Age), grey power, silver surfers, pensioner power; no longer 'golden oldies' or 'old-age pensioners': in today's society the over-60s are a vibrant force to be reckoned with.

As the population ages – by 2010 the majority of British people will be over 50 – if for no other reason than weight of numbers, our potential for influencing society for good becomes ever greater.

If we are to be colour-coded, like a wallpaper or paint chart, has grey become the new red?

It seems to me that retirement is one of those commonly used words well past its sell-by date, for it does not at all accurately describe the very active lives that the majority of post-work people lead. It is, in fact, a time that may well turn out to be the most satisfying, fulfilling and peace-filled period of life: a stage when many tasks and responsibilities can be laid aside, allowing energies to be concentrated upon those things we have always dreamed of doing. It is a time for coming to terms with those ambitions and dreams that now, in all probability, will not be fulfilled and laying them to rest. Also, as mentioned in the Foreword, it is a time for coming to terms with the past and anticipating God's future.

The Oxford English Reference Dictionary (OUP, 1996) offers a variety of meanings for 'retired', all of which are about withdrawal from active involvement, so, do we need a different word to replace the term? How about grey as an alternative? Is this *really* the colour that most closely personifies and represents this richly experienced, vibrant, knowledgeable, wise and resourceful group? Please do not misunderstand me; I would certainly not decry the colour in itself – the soft tones of silver, grey or white hair can look absolutely wonderful, for example – but can it serve as a description of *people*?

I turn to my dictionary again: 'grey: of a colour intermediate between black and white, as of ashes or lead; (of a person) depressed . . . anonymous, nondescript, unidentifiable . . . grey economy: the part of the economy not accounted for in official statistics . . .' These are just a few of the definitions of grey, all of which conjure up somewhat bleak images, so at variance with the reality.

Silver and white fare little better as descriptions of people with a lifetime of experience, so perhaps we need to identify a new colour to symbolise this large and important section of the community. Which would *you* choose? What single colour do you feel best represents and personifies your personality, you as a person? Or do you, like me, feel that one colour alone could not possibly define all the different aspects and complexities that make us what we are; and, for that, we need all the colours of the rainbow?

To turn to the dictionary again, we read: 'rainbow (noun): an arch of colours – red, orange, yellow, green, blue, indigo, violet – formed in the sky opposite the sun by reflection . . . and dispersion of the sun's rays in falling rain, or in spray or mist; (adjective): a wide variety of things . . .'

Applied to a person, then, 'rainbow' speaks of diversity, someone with a wide variety of related experiences and facets. S/he is a reflection of the many experiences of all shades and hues – gathered on the journey through life – that have coloured personality, temperament and attitude. All this wisdom and experience, gained over a lifetime, is of inestimable importance and value to local communities and to the wider society, and it is a tragic loss if it is not harvested and used.

The analogy of a rainbow is developed in a marvellous book by Father Carlos Valles SJ called *I Am Collecting Rainbows*. In the Foreword, titled 'Chasing the Rainbow', he says: 'I set about writing this book as a study in self-integration. When I finished it I realised I had written my autobiography. The result amused me, but was not unexpected. The only way for me to speak on self-integration was to reflect on the way I'd gone about my own integration in my own life.'

Father Valles quotes the philosopher, Martin Heidegger: 'Every man is born as many men and dies as a single one.' He goes on to identify fourteen strands or 'colours', beginning with 'I am many people,' and ending with 'I am I,' which together make up the rainbow of his life.

Perhaps, in imitation of Father Carlos Valles, we need to identify the rainbow colours of our own lives. Then maybe, in the light of the glowing shades we discover, we might radically re-evaluate them, especially if we feel that our life has not yielded that much excitement.

Of course we need to remember that however well we reproduce the colours of our lives, they are provisional, because each minute, each hour, each day we are adding to the picture, a picture that will finally be completed only when we move from this life to the next.

The rainbow was the very powerful and deeply moving image that God chose to describe his constancy and commitment to humankind:

And God said:
'This is the sign of the covenant
I am making between me and you
and every living creature with you,
a covenant for all generations to come.
I have set my rainbow in the clouds
and it will be the sign of the covenant
between me and the earth . . .
This is the sign of the covenant
I have established between me
and all life on the earth.'

(Genesis 9:12-13, 17b)

Then God said:
'This is one
I made before,
in order to
show you how.
Now, go.
Make
your *own*
Rainbow.'

God,
you are the Celestial Artist,
shaping, moulding,
painting in
your rainbow shades
and colouring
the whole of Creation.
I, too, am a miracle,
for I am one
of your works
of art.

A time of all-change

There are times in our lives when everything feels as if it is shifting and changing, with all the familiar and fixed points jolting out of synchronisation. Sometimes, the effect can seem so seismic that we don't recognise any of the landscape any more. It is as if our personal kaleidoscope has taken a sudden turn and produced patterns bewilderingly different from those that have framed our life until that point. All that we can see is that what has been is no more, and this can be very unsettling and painful. We want to cling on to what was and to the familiar.

But endings imply also beginnings. It may be a cliché, but it is nonetheless true that when one door closes another invariably opens – and who knows what promise and opportunity await us on the other side. To find out, we must have the courage, when we feel we are ready, to let go of what has been and to step over the threshold into our future, with all its possibilities and potential – a potential that will only unfold as we live it and experience it. As we do so, we must never forget that God goes with us.

In the Bible, at each exodus or seismic change, we read how the people concerned were told to remember all that God had been in their lives up until then. The Israelites, for example, had to let go of the familiar and step out into the desert and an uncertain future. As the Bible tells us, however, God never left them. He was there constantly and faithfully. So it will be for us, too.

By day the Lord went ahead of them
in a pillar of cloud to guide them on their way
and by night
in a pillar of fire to give them light.

(Exodus 13:21)

12

'All change!'
the guard cried.
'End of the line!'
I must have heard those words
countless times
and paid scant attention to them.
But on my final working days,
they have such a poignant sound.

It is said that when one door shuts,
another opens.
But this is a time of all-change
and there are so many closures to cope with
that all I can see are endings.

When the time is right, Lord,
hold open the doors to my future.
Take my hand and lead me through.
Show me your horizons.
Direct my gaze
and widen my vision,
so I may see all that you
have planned for me.

Help me to unclasp my fingers;
to release my grip;
to softly, gently, tenderly bid farewell
to what I must leave behind.
Give me the courage to reach out
to the future with open hands
and welcome all
that is yet to come.

As one door closes,
another opens.
An ending implies also a beginning:
an open doorway of promise
and of opportunity.
Walk through it with me.

Bless this beginning, Lord.

Open my eyes to see
all the possibilities
that are there to be taken.
Then open my mind
and my heart
to use them aright.

Pillar of fire and cloud,
through the night
and through the day
lead me on.
Whether in desert or fertile times,
you have always been there for me,
leading me on.

And so,
this I know,
to the very depths of my soul,
that you will bring me safe
to the Other Side.

Being joy-full

An inner well of joy that bubbles over into life-giving laughter must surely be one of the most godly ways in which we can gift others. And the ability to laugh at ourselves or with others, however bad things seem, can bring the sun back into dark situations, helping us to move on and restore balance and perspective.

Of course, there is a world of difference between someone who is doggedly, teeth-grittingly jolly, no matter what, and someone who seems always to be sustained by a quiet, inner joy regardless of the situation. The former can grate and seem inappropriate, or even in bad taste, whilst the latter can be a constant source of strength for those who come into contact with such a person.

To have a permanent inner joy is not a denial of the gravity of things. It is, rather, an awareness of God's love breaking through the darkest clouds. To be joy-full is to be hope-full.

On more than one occasion I have been asked whether, since the Bible does not record Jesus ever laughing, laughter is meant to be part of a Christian's expression of their faith. 'Maybe there is no record', I replied, 'because the Gospel writers assumed we could not possibly truly experience the love of God in Jesus Christ without the joy of that reality overflowing in delight.'

The ability to laugh is uniquely human. It is a God-given way for us to express delight and joy. Laughter, it has been proved, can activate both the mental and physical healing processes. A decision for a laughter- and joy-filled life even in the face of adversity is, therefore, a choice for healing and wholeness.

> Be joyful always . . .
> for this is God's will for you
> in Christ Jesus.
> (1 Thessalonians 5:16, 18b)

Jesus,
it's not easy,
is it,
always to be full of joy,
even when the sun
has gone –
to keep hope alive
and bright,
when hopelessness rules
the day?
I've come to the conclusion
that it
has little necessarily to do
with inclination,
but much with self-discipline.

I want to be a source
of strength
for those whose lives
touch mine.
To bring light and life
into dark situations,
rather than adding to the sum
of sorrows.
I want to decide for
a laughter-filled,
a joy-filled life,
even in the face
of adversity.

Only with your help
can I do it.
Stay close by.
Live your joy and hope
in me.

Dear God,
how can you speak of *joy*
when my life
is so torn apart?

Laugh?
I feel more like screaming
with the pain inside.

Help me.

Open my heart.

Break through into my darkness
and despair.
Warm me with your life-giving
rays of light.

Heavenly Father,
'Be joyful always'.
We are told
this is your will for us,
in Christ Jesus.

More than anything
I want to live out your commands.

'Be joyful always.'
If this is what you want
of me,
how can I
do other?

Developing a holistic spirituality

Hopefully, as we move through life, we recognise more and more the importance of discovering who it is we really are and of being true to what we find. A consequence of this self-discovery is the sense of release and freedom that is generated, one aspect of which is feeling increasingly able to step beyond the conformities of belief and behaviour that institutions – whether they are church or society – impose.

Having the courage radically to explore one's faith and, from that search, to craft a personal spirituality into which is woven the understanding born of life experience, can release us to 'know' God in profound new ways. Consequently, far from our faith becoming more conservative as we grow older, we are opened up to ever-deeper mysteries of the divine. God becomes at once closer than a heartbeat and yet, at the same time, more shrouded and unknowable.

As we become ever more aware of God's presence permeating every part of his Creation, our prayer life will change automatically, in response.

Jesus said to the man:
'Stretch out your hand.'
He did so, and his hand was completely restored . . .
Jesus went out to a mountainside to pray,
and spent the night praying to God.
When morning came,
he called his disciples to him
and chose twelve of them,
whom he also designated apostles . . .
Then a great crowd came to hear him
and to be healed of their diseases . . .'
(Luke 6:10b, 12b-13, 17b, 18a)

Jesus,
there is a disintegration
in my life.
On the one hand,
there are all the day-by-day things
that I endeavour to do
in your Name:
the caring and the sharing
and the loving.
On the other,
here is my life of prayer.
Both are as essential to me
as the air I breathe.
Yet I look at your way of being
and of doing,
and I see what a difference there is
between me and you.
Your prayer life
formed a seamless whole
with everything else that you did.
Not even the sharpest of blades
could get between the two.
Help me to pull myself together.
Make a seamless robe
of my life:
a celestial garment
worthy of a follower of you.

Jesus,
'holistic':
it's a fashionable word these days,
not only in the world of spirituality,
but on business training days
and in the boardrooms, too.
Has the concept been hijacked –
cynical commercial use
made of the holy –
or is there a genuine attempt
at integration
of body, mind and spirit?

You always worked with the ways
of the world
when you walked this earth.
Taking the everyday,
reinterpreting,
and thereby transforming it.
Is all of this
part of your mighty plan?

What we constantly say,
eventually becomes what we are.
Are you encouraging work jargon
to mimic the language of
'God-speak'
for your own ends?
Are you entering into minds and hearts
through the eyes of the world?

Use me, Lord.
Train me in your methods.
May my words and how I use them,
my actions and how I do them,
tell of integration.
May all that I am,
speak to others of a new way of being;
directing them to you.

Facing loss of various kinds

Whenever someone mentions loss in a human context, our minds naturally turn to bereavement. But, of course, we can experience a profound sense of loss with regard to anything that has been important or precious to us, especially that which cannot be replaced or experienced again. Examples are many: when we move from one stage of life to another, such as from work to retirement, or when the last child leaves the family home; loss of status, when we give up a position that has commanded respect or that has identified us as a particular type of person; loss of independence, through such things as ill-health or age; decreasing eyesight, hearing, hair, mental or physical mobility; and lessening ability to remember names, places or detail as quickly as we once did. We prize long life, but we dread its diminishments.

The latter part of life particularly is a time when losses are not necessarily replaced and the awareness of this can compound the sadness and grief felt. The key to restoring happiness at these times is the way we face our losses. We need to be adaptable, investing in other activities and relationships to take the place of those that we have no longer.

At these times it's so important also to remind ourselves that, in God's eyes, our worth is not defined by what we *do* but by what we *are*. These moments can be instances of real grace, when we are able to accept our diminishments with patience, stoicism and that blessed thing, a sense of humour.

Losses challenge our faith and bring us face to face with what we believe. Do we see God primarily as the cause of our suffering, or as a source of strength in dealing with it?

> When I was brought low,
> God gave me strength.
> My heart, be at peace once again.
> (Psalm 116:6b, 7a)

Heavenly Father,
may my days be many
and may I value and treasure
all that is in them.
I do prize long life
but I dread the infirmities
that advancing years may bring.
How shall I cope should they strike?
Will they make me a burden to others?
Such fears haunt me.
Thank you for your promise
of constancy.
Whatever the future may hold,
I place it all
in your hands.
If the moments of my worst fears
are realised,
give me your courage
to face them.
Within each limitation,
new opportunities and blessings
are waiting to be born.
Help me to seek
and to find you there.
May I accept whatever may come
with your grace
and without fear.

Loving Lord,
thank you for what we had.

Thank you for what we shared.

Thank you that I knew such love.

When the pain has gone,
when the healing is complete,
may no memory of this sadness
stop me from opening myself up
to loving again.

Jesus,
I cannot believe it is no longer
in my life,
shaping it, framing it,
filling it to the horizon
with its presence.

Now it has gone,
there's this great emptiness
where once it was –
yet the space is somehow filled
with grief and with pain.

Draw near,
tender Lord.
Hold me close.
Soothe this terrible ache of loss.

Lord,
each profound experience
irrevocably changes us.
I'm not the same person I was
before this happened.
I'm at a new starting point,
learning how and where
I go from here.
Walk with me,
Jesus.
Guide the new steps I have to take.
Teach me
what I need to learn.
Help me to turn this loss
into gain.
And may it all be
to your greater glory.

For all it's worth

I remember, when I was in my mid-teens, thinking that anyone over 25 years of age was well on the road to being old. I could not picture myself at such an advanced age. I had such a sense of urgency that everything I wanted to do and to achieve had to be packed in before this deadline – and it did seem, literally, a 'dead' line. Of course, as I moved towards this 'dead' line, it shifted to a convenient point some years ahead, this process being repeated as I went through my early years.

Some of the losses older people experience stem not from the ageing process but from the attitudes of younger people towards ageing. Older people present younger ones with a picture of what they might become that they cannot comprehend and a reality that they probably prefer not to contemplate – the fact that they too, one day, will no longer be young.

Mature people, in their turn, can look with wistful longing at young people; lives stretching before them, dreams not yet compromised, boundless amounts of energy and opportunity, and so on.

However, each stage of life brings its own special opportunities. It is so important, as we grow older, to cultivate an appreciation and discernment of what each day can bring – and then to live it, for all we are worth.

Jesus said:
'I tell you,
do not worry about your life.
Who of you,
by worrying,
can add a single hour
to your life?'

(Matthew 6:25a, 27)

Jesus,
you taught,
'Do not worry about yesterday,
nor about tomorrow,
but live each day as it comes.'
What is it about
our human condition
that we find it so very hard
to focus the whole of our attention
on *this* moment,
this *now*,
and upon no other?
Is it an avoidance tactic –
a kind of dreaming
to take us away
from our responsibility
for today?
How often,
knowing there is so much to do,
do I delay the moment of engaging with the present
by worrying about the future,
or agonising over the past?
Yet your words
are unequivocal and clear:
'Give your entire attention
to what God is doing right now,
and don't get worked up
about what may –
or may not –
happen tomorrow.
God will help you deal
with whatever hard things come up
when the time comes.'

(based on Matthew 6:34)

Lord,
help me to live today
for all it's worth.

The old wood of yesterday
and the raw shoots
of tomorrow,
each have their place
in my thoughts.

But the past has gone
and the future
is yet to come.
And this present day,
this *now*,
is my only reality.

So, Lord,
help me to live today,
for all it's worth.

Generous God,
our lives are precious gifts
from you,
parables of Talents
not to be buried.
So help me to value
and to treasure
each bright new day
with all its possibilities
and potential,
from this day forward
until my life's end.

From fear to love

'Do not be afraid,' the angel says to Mary, when he comes to speak of the birth of the Messiah. Similarly, 'Do not be afraid', are the first words Jesus speaks to his disciples when he appears to them after his resurrection.

These four words occur so frequently in the Bible – something like once for every day of the year – that the message must be one of which we are to take serious note.

For some people, the ageing process can become a fear-filled one as they are confronted with the various diminishments and limitations that gradually come upon us as we grow older. Fear can cripple us more surely than any physical illness for, unless checked, it can insinuate itself like a fast-growing weed into every area of our lives and overwhelm us. So, it is probably no coincidence that we are challenged as Christians to move from a fear-driven to a love-motivated life.

God is love.
When we take up permanent residence
in a life of love,
we live in God and God lives in us . . .
There is no room in love for fear.
Well-formed love banishes fear.
Since fear is crippling, a fearful life –
fear of death, fear of judgement –
is not yet fully formed in love.

(1 John 4:16b, 18)

Jesus,
I read your words,
'Do not be afraid',
and I wonder
if what you say
can be directed also
particularly at me?

I don't see myself as a fearful person.
Yet is that *truly* so?
Your words have struck a chord.
They have challenged me.
Now I look deeply and honestly inward
and I come face to face
with so many subtle fears,
that chain me down
and hold me back
with fine silken threads
invisible to my former casual gaze.

Then, a revelation:
it is not my smallness
but my potential
that I most profoundly fear,
because once I admit
that not even the sky is the limit
for what I can achieve
in the power of your Name,
then I have no reason
for not reaching for the stars –
and beyond –
in order to realise
your dreams for me:
my destiny called out
to your greater glory.

Tender God,
when I was overwhelmed with fear,
you gave me the courage to turn,
to face
and to go through it.

Now my heart is at peace again.
Thank you
for your faithful love.

Jesus,
this is the time for which
I have so often longed.
But now it is reality,
my main emotions
are bewilderment and fear.
The old routine
filled and framed my days
and took away the need to decide.
Now it is no longer there
and I must take responsibility
for how I use all this time
at my disposal.
Help me to make wise choices.
Help me to see it all
as the beginning
of an exciting new chapter –
and not just the ending
of the one before.

Loving God,
may I be so filled with love –
for you
and for all whom I meet –
that fear becomes a thing
of the past,
never more to limit the present.

Giving thanks in all circumstances

Perhaps one of the most challenging statements in the whole Bible is the directive to 'give thanks in all circumstances'. Clearly, the ability to be thankful even in the bad and sad times is profoundly spiritual, as well as deeply religious. The two have to go hand in hand.

To be spiritual is not necessarily to be religious, and vice versa. 'I give thanks to God, even in this bad time', is a deeply religious statement. However, to *be*, and to *feel*, thankful, is profoundly *spiritual*.

It can seem extremely perverse to be thankful in the face of pain and loss, as if, in doing so, we are in denial of the seriousness and effect of that pain or loss. However, if God is in all things, then he must necessarily be present in our sorrow as well as our joy; indeed, probably *more* present then than at any other time.

We need also to see the bad and sad times against the backdrop of our lives in their entirety. One of the advantages of age is that we have had more time to learn that most bad things are of a temporary nature. We learn to say, 'Time passes. This, also, will pass.' And, if it doesn't pass, but proves to be permanent, then, hopefully, we have also had time in which to learn, through personal experience, of God's faithfulness: 'at all times and in all places'.

Thank God, no matter what happens.
This is the way God wants you
who belong to Christ Jesus
to live.

(1 Thessalonians 5:18)

36

Jesus,
I think of your worst circumstance –
the Cross –
and I wonder:
Did you give thanks,
even then?
In the midst
of all your pain,
and sorrow at what had been done –
at the moment
you cried out,
'My God! My God!
Why have you forsaken me?' –
were you giving thanks,
even then?
Did you gasp out
the first words
of that psalm,
not in accusation,
but as a thanksgiving?
Did you offer the beginning
of that song of praise
to a faithful God who,
however dark the valley,
always stoops to listen –
who never abandons those
that cry out to him
from the depths
of their despair?

(The reference here is to Psalm 22)

Heavenly Father,
I thank you for the good.
In obedience,
I thank you
for the bad
and pray that good may come
from it.
Give me the faith
to believe it will.
Give me the steadfastness
and courage I need,
during the times
of waiting.

Jesus,
your light shines through
even the darkest cloud.
I thank you
and I praise you,
now
and always.

Lord,
I sit by her bedside
and watch and listen
as her life on earth
ebbs away.
I think
and I remember.
And I thank you
for all
we have shared.

Growing old, graciously and gracefully

One of my first childhood memories was of my grandmother, seated in her garden, shelling peas. The sun was shining, the roses she tended and loved filling the air with their scent and colour. My grandmother's whole manner was of a peaceful person, at home in this time in her life.

Her earlier years had seen much adventure and variety, and she had lived abroad, in very challenging circumstances, for a number of years.

Although I was too young, at that time, to be aware of her history, I remember instinctively recognising and feeling her quiet, dignified strength of character, rock-like stability and dependability. She had also retained all of her considerable elegance and femininity, had a walk that a model might have envied and possessed a delicious sense of mischievousness and fun, which often resulted in her crying with laughter. She had grown old, graciously and gracefully and with a real sense of style.

Age had not diminished but, rather, accentuated the things of enduring value.

Her whole life had been directed and sustained by a deep and rock-like faith which, at the end, was reflected in her choice of hymn for her funeral: 'O Love that wilt not let me go'. It was an infinitely important model for a 4-year-old child to internalise.

God said:
'I shall direct you
and show you
the way
to go.
I shall not take my eyes
off you.'

(Psalm 32:8)

Jesus,
I bring you my life's gifts.

Gold:
for the wealth of experience.
Riches accumulated,
that are too many
to reckon.

Frankincense:
for all the heartfelt prayers
of a lifetime.
Holy smoke,
rising like incense
as you stoop to listen.

Myrrh:
for all the sad,
the bad times.
Bitter aloes made sweet,
because it was then
you carried me.

Creator God,
my autumn leaves are fallen
and my summer flowers have disappeared
and the earth that is my body lies wrinkled
with the age of the year.

Now is the sacrament
of my winter season,
that I offer up to you.

But beneath the soil,
where I cannot see,
I know spring seeds lie
waiting,
shaping,
growing,
into their yet-to-be.

Faithful God,
through all the twists
and turns
of my life,
you have guided me.
Whenever I lost
my sense of direction,
you showed me
the way
that I should go.
God of love,
stay very close.
Do not take your eyes
off me.

Help me to grow old,
graciously,
gracefully.
May I live my life
in a way that
nurtures and sustains others.
But above all else,
may it be
pleasing to you,
my Saviour,
my Comforter,
my Friend.

Hard times

One of the most well-known but difficult to comprehend sayings of Jesus is, 'My yoke is easy and my burden is light'. Jesus' burden *light*? Can this *really* be so for the Saviour of the world, who offers to carry all its cares on his shoulders?

A yoke is shaped to make bearing loads easier by dispersing the weight along its length rather than it being concentrated at certain pressure points. I wonder whether Jesus was giving us a centrally important lesson about the way in which we manage *all* the obligations, responsibilities and preoccupations of the everyday, not just when the everyday becomes burdensome.

Despite his demanding and punishing schedule, Jesus, so we gather from the Gospels, kept his life in perfect balance. However hectic his days, he made time to pray; to be so aware of the needs of others that he could sense someone touching the hem of his garment in the hope of being healed; and he made time to relax at meals and parties with both friends and strangers. He kept in close touch with his inner self and his needs.

Prayer, however, was his life force; a wellspring he drew on constantly, particularly before some demanding task or when times were hard.

Jesus said:
'Come to me, all you who are weary and burdened,
and I will give you rest.
Take my yoke upon you and learn from me,
for I am gentle and humble in heart,
and you will find rest for your souls.
For my yoke is easy
and my burden is light.'
(Matthew 11:28-30)

Jesus,
when you said,
'Blessed are you
who are poor',
I know your words were meant
to comfort and console.
But they don't pay the bills.

I know, too,
you were speaking
of poverty of spirit,
rather than in financial terms.

But it's true,
nonetheless,
that you are there,
at the epicentre of my worries,
sharing them all with me,
whatever they may be.

Guide me
to make the most
of what I have:
money,
talents,
gifts of other kinds.
Help me
to 'spend' it all wisely
and with discernment.

Saviour,
I remember your words
of comfort and strength
and I reach out
for your hand.

Your clasp is firm.
When times are hard,
or when I am weary and weak,
then truly you are able to be
at your strongest
within me.

Thank you for your tender care.

Thank you
for your great and constant love.

Jesus!
Please help me.

I *can't* go on like this.

Shoulder my load.

It is too heavy
for me to bear.

Generous God,
I may be poorer
than I was
in financial terms,
but I am rich
in all that really matters.
Thank you
for so abundantly
blessing me.

Harvesting memories

Would you class yourself as a pessimist, or an optimist? Or, to put it in a slightly different way, do you normally perceive containers filled to 50 per cent of their capacity as half empty or half full?

Many a highly successful comedy film and TV programme has been built around characters who insist on seeing everything in its worst possible light, their attitude to life setting in motion an often hilarious chain of consequences.

We can do much the same when remembering the past: only the bad is recalled, often as justification for a negative outlook on life that calls forth a kind of cynical, know-it-all, 'I told you so' attitude.

The most contented older people frequently seem to be those who make a habit of harvesting good memories and filling the storehouses of their minds with them. These memories provide a rich repository of resources, ready to be drawn upon, as needed, for nourishment. It is not that the lives of these people have necessarily been easier or more privileged than the average. Rather, their contentment speaks of an attitude to life, a self-discipline, which insists upon finding the creative and special within every situation, however negative or ordinary, and making a deliberate choice to remember and affirm that.

Memories can also be explored in order to shed light upon the past, the present and the future. This can result in profound new understandings that alter current perceptions of who and what a person is, of situations and of the variety of options that are consequently open.

Give thanks to the Lord . . .
Sing praise to him;
tell of all his wonderful acts . . .
Remember the wonders he has done,
his miracles . . .
(1 Chronicles 16:8a, 9b, 12a)

Redeeming God,
I look back
and I remember.
I survey
the people and the events
that have coloured my life
and how I responded
in each situation;
what opportunities
I took up
and those I let
pass me by.

Wheat and tares,
good and bad:
there they are,
growing together,
intertwined
and impossible to separate.

But I am at peace
with that.
How often my life has shown
that good has somehow come
out of bad:
your redemption at work
in the detail.

I gather my harvest
into the storehouses
of my mind and my heart.
There they will stay;
rich resources
to draw on
in the lean times,
when I need nourishment.

Tender God,
through a glass darkly
is how I see my past –
and it's colouring
all my memories.

When I look back
all I see is sadness.

But buried in there,
somewhere,
must be good things
that have become overlaid
by the sands of hard times.

Help me to search
and to find them.

They are my buried treasure.

Jesus,
help me to remember
those times,
situations
and encounters,
that are special
to you.

Then show me how
I may use them,
to inform
my present
and my future.

Healing rifts

One of the best things about growing older is our ever-increasing awareness of the value of time. Relationships that have turned sour, or that have drifted apart – maybe through misunderstandings or lack of nurture, or for some other reason – may now be seen in a different perspective.

When we are young, we can feel that there is all the time in the world for some things, yet immense pressure on time in other ways. Often, we are unsure how to resolve certain situations and so we put them on hold, to be dealt with at some vague future date. Time passes and other preoccupations assume greater importance. We can also allow our perception of justice in a given situation to cloud the picture: 'I didn't start it,' we argue, 'so why should I take the first step to heal things?'

As we grow older, we hopefully grow wiser and increasingly realise that healing broken relationships is what counts most, issues of 'justice' being of secondary importance.

As part of freeing up our lives and ourselves, we do well to reflect on where relationships are suffering from unresolved conflicts or hurts, and then to reach out across the rift in love and forgiveness. Such individual acts of generosity of spirit cannot help but affect society as a whole for the good.

> Forgive us our sins,
> as we forgive those
> that sin against us.
>
> (Matthew 6:12)

Healing Lord,
it is so hard,
yet again,
to take the first step
to resolve things,
when *I* was not the one
who started it all.
I've tried so often before
to make things right,
but my advances
have always been rejected.
Each time,
I feel I am being further disadvantaged.
And yet . . .
and yet,
I can't bear for it to carry on like this.
There's heartache
if I do nothing,
and there's heartache
of a different kind,
if my efforts are turned away.
'Forgive us our sins,
as we forgive
those that sin against us.'
Your words haunt
and challenge me.
They bring me face to face
with what it is
I have to do.
Walk with me.
Give me the grace
and the words I need
to try again,
and this time,
I beg of you,
may healing be the result.

I want to be free,
Lord.
Free from all the things
that hold me back
and pin me down
into the past.
I've let go of bad memories,
and sadnesses that erode
my sense of well-being.
Now I turn my attention
to relationships.
Of all the precious things
you have blessed me with,
surely these come at the top of the list.
Open my eyes
to any offence or hurts
to anyone
that I have inadvertently inflicted
by thought,
or word,
or deed,
so that I can endeavour to make right
any wrongs,
before it is too late.

Thank you,
healing Saviour,
for bringing dying relationships
back to life;
for the gentle touch
of your hands
in each and every situation,
no matter how hopeless
these may seem.

Holy hands

It is said that you can always tell the real age of a person by their hands. Face or body nips and tucks can pretend to a different age, but hands speak the story as it really is: each blemish and wrinkle a true life-line. And what a history they can tell: hands that may have reached out in generosity, friendship and love; been clenched in anxiety and anger; tenderly yet respectfully held the trusting fingers of a child; soothed away pain; hurt someone with their heavy-handedness; wiped away tears, whether of others or of the individual themselves; touched evil; or clasped together in prayers of thanksgiving, entreaty and praise.

It is these same hands, life-worn and life-stained, that we hold out to receive the transforming bread of Christ's body. How important it is, then, for us to do all we can to ensure that our hands reflect the example of Jesus' hands, and that our touch on life is holy, like his.

One will say,
'I belong to the Lord' . . .
another will write on his hand,
'The Lord's' . . .

(Isaiah 44:5)

56

Jesus,
my hands are life-worn
and life-stained.
Some of the marks are holy.
Some of them record truths
that make me bow my head
in shame.

It is these same hands –
life-worn and life-stained
and containing my story –
that I hold out like a cup,
to be made holy
by the transforming bread
of your body.

And as I do,
I think of your hands
reaching out:
giving,
touching,
healing,
raising,
eternally scarred
with the marks of your glory;
writing in the dust of the earth
and telling your story
of a love
beyond
description.

Saviour,
I imagine the feel
of my hand
in yours.
My trembling fingers
encased
and held firm
in your strong
and steady
grasp.

When I reach out
in fear,
you are there
ready,
waiting only for me to ask,
before instantly reaching back
to touch me
in my need.

What would I do
without you?
How could I live
without you?
Where would I turn
if not to your love?
You are my Strength.
You are my Life.

Father,
hands are surely
one of the miracles of your Creation.
Thank you for my hands.
May my touch on life
be tender and life-giving.

Increasing physical limitations

The well-known, at once humorous and touching prayer of a nun in which she asks God to give her the grace not to lovingly rehearse her increasing aches and pains, but to concentrate all her energies out towards the needs of others, must strike a chord with many people. In a similar vein, the active and vociferous protests by elderly, often wheelchair-bound residents of nursing homes threatened with closure, offer examples of people who refuse to let their increasing infirmities get in the way of what they want, plan or are determined to do.

Alongside these can be placed the old lady who, having never flown before, chose to celebrate her 100th birthday with a flight on the world's fastest passenger plane.

Add, too, the 58-year-old man with inoperable cancer who, when he heard the prognosis, listed all the things he'd ever dreamed of doing – from white-water rafting on some of the most dangerous and fast-flowing runs, to visiting his brother in Africa and going on safari – and managed to realise all these dreams before he died.

All these people, in their profound celebration of life, are testimony to the power of mind over matter and the indomitability of the human spirit.

To continue to set goals, whatever our age or physical condition, is extremely important to our mental well-being, as it lifts our vision to the horizons of our possibilities. Whether we actually manage to achieve these goals is of secondary importance.

However limited physically we become, there is always something we can do. One of the most important things we can do for others is to pray for them; something that requires no physical input at all.

I look up to the mountains;
but does my strength come from mountains?
No,
my strength comes from God,
who made heaven
and earth
and mountains.

(Psalm 121:1-2)

Eternal God,
there seems to be an inverse correlation
between my plans
and goals
and my physical capability
to put them into effect.
For every thing achieved,
for every dream realised,
it seems as though
two take their place.
So here I am,
with an ever-expanding list
of things I long to do,
and with an ever-shrinking
physical ability to do them.
I've come to the conclusion
that there are two ways
to view this state of affairs:
either I despair,
or else I celebrate the fact
that my mind grows ever more able
to soar like a bird.
I recall the words of your prophet,
as he proclaimed your glory:
'[God] gives strength to the weary,
and increases the power of the weak . . .
those who hope in the Lord
will renew their strength.
They will soar on wings like eagles:
they will run and not grow weary,
they will walk and not be faint.'
I place my hope in you.
I know you will give me the strength
for those dreams you want me to fulfil in life.
Glory be to you, O Lord,
my power and my strength.

(the reference here is to Isaiah 40:29, 31)

Jesus,
thank you for my mind which,
despite the physical restrictions
of my body,
still is sharp as the proverbial razor
and as stubborn as ever it was.
With that,
I can climb any mountains of obstacles
that get in the way
of what I determine to do.
I remember what you said about mountains:
that if we had faith
the size of a mustard seed
we could move them,
according to our wish and will,
from one place to another.
The smallest of seeds
that grows into the largest of plants;
what a wonderful analogy
with which to challenge and to inspire.
So, Lord,
my prayer is simply this:
that you will give me
the strength of belief
the size of a mustard seed.

I praise you,
Lord,
from whom all blessings flow.
You are my strength.
In you there is all the freedom
in the world –
and beyond.

Laying aside illusions and false expectations

Autumn is a time, in nature, when the leaves fall from their branches and we are able to see more clearly the amazing and wondrous complexity of the trees' basic structure, yet to appreciate the uniqueness of each one: some branches reaching towards the heavens whilst others droop towards the earth that has nurtured them. As the outer covering falls away, we are confronted with the inner reality. We are made much more aware that the tree has become what it has fed from.

So it is with us, as we grow and mature. What we are now is shaped and moulded by the choices we have made in the past: the particular events and situations that were visited upon us may not always have been of our choosing, but our attitudes and responses were.

When we are young, we dream of what we might one day be. As we grow older and look back, there can seem little connection between the reality and some, or many, of those youthful and fanciful dreams. So it is good that we take time to reflect with honesty and humility upon what we have become.

We need to sift through our dreams and gently to place into God's keeping our illusions and false hopes about ourselves. Then, stripped back of all that is unnecessary, we may grow more purposefully towards the future God wills for and holds out to us.

Jesus said: 'I am the true vine and my Father is the gardener.
He cuts off every branch in me that bears no fruit,
whilst every branch that does bear fruit,
he prunes so that it will be even more fruitful.'
(John 15:1-2)

Tender God –
it is so hard to let go
of the dreams
that I know now
will not come to pass.
It feels as though an integral part of me
will disappear when they go.
Help me to loosen my grip.
Such moments of realisation
are periods of real grief,
for these dreams have sustained and taken me
through some very low times.
They have helped me
to feel good about myself
and about the future,
by lifting my eyes
to wondrous and new possibilities.
Help me to loosen my grip.
For now I can see
that it's time for me
to unclench my mind
and to let the illusions drift away
on the gentle winds of time.
Only when my head is clear
can I begin to replace
the old with the new.
Help me to loosen my grip.
Show me the dreams
you have for me,
so that I may grow
into your Reality,
rather than be limited
by my own.

Creator God,
before you made the world,
did you dream it into existence
in your mind?
Were your dreams a precursor
of all that then became real?
Before I was born,
what did you dream for me?
Have I,
in any way, shape or form,
come up to any of your expectations?
Life becomes more and more precious
with every passing day;
no time for illusions or false expectations,
taking me off the course
you have set for me.
Dream your dreams in me.
Then help me to bring them to life.

Heavenly Father,
some things are so different
from how I once pictured they would be.
Others have surpassed expectation,
and yet others are consequences –
some good and some bad –
of choices and decisions made.
I can see,
much clearer than ever before,
who I really am.
The illusions seem to have fallen away
of their own accord.
It's as though you are pruning
and shaping me for my future.
May it be fruitful
and worthy of your Harvest.

Laying aside regrets

Throughout our lives, memories surface that need to be faced and integrated into our present if we are to be at peace with ourselves. Some of these memories most probably will be precious and treasured. Others may feel like a knife twisting in our hearts each time they are recalled.

Our past, with its mixture of success and failure, happiness and sorrow, pain and joy, selfishness and love, is what has shaped and moulded us into what we are now.

It is easy and often delightful to reflect upon and revel in the good, the happy recollections. But it is very tempting to push the bad memories out of sight and to try to forget that they were ever part of us. It can take a great deal of courage to *choose* to look back at that which has been painful or destructive for us.

However, such memories can hold us in bondage, without us realising it, so, if we are to be truly free, we need to make a conscious decision to face and address them.

Shining the light of our present knowledge and wisdom on to our memories of the past can be very powerful in helping to heal sad or hurtful memories. It is a task, though, that we may have to undertake a number of times before we can declare ourselves truly healed. When this has been done, we are more able to live the present moment to its full potential and to look forward to all that is to come, unburdened by those things in our past that have been negative for us.

A 'yes' to our past transforms itself into a 'yes' to our present and to our future.

It is for freedom that Christ has set us free.
Stand firm then,
and do not let yourselves be burdened again
by the yoke of slavery.

(Galatians 5:1)

Jesus,
there are so many things I regret:
roads not taken
and opportunities missed,
because I was looking the other way –
or could not recognise the signs
for what they were.

Please help me to lay
my sadness aside.
to trust that maybe –
just maybe –
the way it all actually happened
was best, after all.
That feeling regretful
will not alter the past,
but may well stop me
seeing the possibilities
in the now
and in what is to come.

Retrospection has its place,
but help me not to be trapped
in my past.
Help me to keep my gaze
fixed on the road ahead;
truly to know that,
in saying 'yes' to my past,
I say 'yes' to my present and future.

Most important of all,
in saying 'yes' to all of that,
I say 'yes'
to you.

Forgiving God,
when I look back,
in the light of what now I know,
there are so many things
I wish I could change:
harsh words spoken in anger,
or kind ones left unsaid;
acting in haste
and regretting at leisure –
or not acting at all.
And so much else, as well.

Forgive the things
that I got wrong.
May they be growth points
leading me
into the future,
rather than sticking points
holding me back
in the past.

Heal my memories,
that I may be healed.

Thank you for the gift
of recollection,
especially about those things
that now I grieve over,
but from which I can learn
so much.

Healing God,
you have answered my prayer,
you have healed my memories,
you have lifted my burden from me.
Now I can look forward to the future,
with a light heart.
I thank you
and I praise you.

Life-lines

What is behind the current preoccupation with denying our real age by allowing someone to inject us with poison – in a practice known as Botoxing – in order to obliterate the lines that tell our life story; why are we so reluctant to carry the signs of having lived beyond our twenties, when it is clear in every other way that we are – well, not as young as once we were?

Artists through the ages most often chose models who were past the first flush of youth, precisely because their life-lines made their features so much more interesting to draw and to paint.

It is very right to want to take care of our bodies and to make them look as good as we can; to nourish and nurture our skin; to dress and to present ourselves attractively; to preserve our youthful strength and vitality with a healthy lifestyle and eating and exercise. After all, our bodies are the temples of the Spirit and a gift from God, which we should treat with respect and reverence.

People who speak out in defence of Botoxing say it is no different from dyeing hair or other interventions. But is that actually so? Would we feel the need or the desire or, indeed, the pressure if our culture were not such a youth-orientated one?

Youth is a wonderful, transient gift, but it is important for us also to remember that there are things beyond a beautiful, unblemished skin. We must keep a sense of perspective. Surface is not enough; we have to have substance, too.

It does seem sad when people feel the need to wipe away every indication of the fact that they have lived a certain number of years. Surely that is, rather, something of which to be proud, for experience, wisdom and age are beautiful, as well.

We need to learn to age gracefully, and with a real sense of style, if we are not to slip into ever-deeper gloom as each new ineradicable wrinkle appears.

The Lord said:
'God does not see the same way people see.
People look at the outside of a person,
but the Lord looks at the heart.' (1 Samuel 16:7b)

Is *this* who I am?
Good Lord!
I'm face to face with myself in the mirror
and it's *not* a pretty sight!
Everything looks to me
to be on a downward shift,
where, once upon a time,
(most) was taut and firm.
No longer does my exterior
match the way I feel inside.
Maybe I've been just too busy to notice –
or to mourn it –
until now.

But, all of a sudden,
it seems so powerfully sign and symbol
of what time has done
and of the years beyond recall.
Help me not to take
an emotional or mental downward drift
along with all the rest of me.
Neither to grieve nor to regret,
but to be full of thanks
for what has gone before.

The lines speak of reality,
of so much to celebrate
as well as to mourn –
of sadness and joy,
success and failure,
loneliness and love,
struggle and achievement,
tears and laughter,
death and birth,
all of them together saying,
'This is me, so far;
this is where I have reached
in my life journey;
THIS IS WHO I AM!

Dear God,
parts of me are sagging
rather more
than they used to do.

Wrinkles,
that I like to call laugh-lines,
are much more evident.

But I see them as trophies;
prizes for years
fully lived.

I'm happy to have them.
They illustrate a story
about me:
who I am now,
as well as all that's
gone before.

It's all a tale,
that only time
can tell.

Jesus,
however grey
I get,
may life
seem
evergreen.

Middle-of-the-road time

When a friend reached her 50th birthday, a fact about which she was feeling very ambivalent, her son remarked reassuringly, 'Just think, Mum, you're half-way to 100!' 'So is this second half-century to be seen as a count-*down* or count-*up* time?' she wondered dismally.

'Mid-life crises' can affect men and women equally. They are often the result of us realising suddenly, with a jolting shock, that there are probably more active days behind us than lie before us. This realisation that there are, in all likelihood, more yesterdays than tomorrows can lead to all sorts of deep searchings, questioning, regrets and even despair if we are not able to come to terms with our lives as they have been.

Those of us who are Christians, with a belief in a life hereafter, are blessed in being able to perceive the latter part of life not as a run-down but as a run-up towards *the* meeting of our lives. However, having such faith is not necessarily a guarantee against the spontaneous everyday fears, doubts, worries and regrets that seem to be part of our natural human condition.

If we *are* able to see this life as a preparation for what is to come, then the later years of our lives take on a different kind of urgency, fuelled not by despair but by a realisation that we no longer have all the time in the world to get ourselves ready for this final encounter.

Hopefully, then, life becomes clearer and more simplified. That which is truly important comes into clearer focus and is sharpened up. We need to use the understanding gained to power us into an exciting future that is full of mystery and promise, and that beckons us ever onward.

It is the paradox of the Christian faith that God makes the desert bloom and clothes dry bones in muscle and flesh. When we are at our lowest is when God can do his most transforming work.

My grace is enough, it's all you need.
My strength comes into its own in your weakness.
(2 Corinthians 12:9a)

Eternal God,
it's not exactly a mid-life *crisis*
I bring before you,
but this particular time
is not too easy.
There are so many endings of things
that called for so much of me –
my love, my energy –
and not enough beginnings
taking their place.
The children are grown and gone,
spreading their young wings
in a beckoning world.
And in the wake of their departure,
I've suddenly realised I'm middle-aged.
I suppose I was too busy
to notice it –
before, I had so much time.
Please help me to open my eyes
and see a world
that is beckoning also to *me*.
It is time for me
to spread *my* wings, as well;
to explore within myself
and to rediscover who I am,
now,
at this moment in my life –
on my own account
and not just in relation to others.

Giver of life,
from this peak
called the middle of my life,
I look back to the first part:
to its highs and lows,
its sorrows and joys.

I can look forward as well –
to an unknown future
spread before me,
like a map without a key
to unlock its secrets.

But I don't want to know
what will be
in the years to come.
I love the excitement of wondering
what lies beyond
my range of vision.

Thank you.
Thank you for the gift
of my life,
with its ever-changing scenery
and its enchanting mystery.

Jesus –
count-down or count-up time:
which will it be for me,
I wonder.

The crown of your life
was your last three years.
It was like the final soaring,
heart-stoppingly beautiful notes
of a piece of music,
that linger in the mind,
and haunt the soul eternally
with their loveliness.

May my life reflect
this crescendo.

More truly ourselves

Society, in the West, is a youth-orientated culture; it might even be said, a youth-worshipping culture.

To appreciate and to value highly the qualities and attributes of the young is essential in a healthy society; after all, the young are the future.

However, it is all too easy for society to be pressurised into internalising these perceptions to such an extent that a youth-affirming society becomes, at the same time, an age-denying society. Then people, as they grow older, feel increasingly that they are being forced into a mould, or way of being, which reflects neither the reality nor their wishes for themselves.

Ancient communities and many societies in the East have much to teach us, in this regard. In these cultures, the older the person becomes the more he or she is venerated for their age and the wisdom that advancing years hopefully bring in their wake.

It is sad that, on the whole, the West has lost this appreciation of the tremendous value and resource of older people to their particular society, not just for their particular gifts but also as a symbol, an icon, of an 'otherness'.

It can be hard to resist internalising the collective or majority views of a community and then, regardless of how you really feel, living down to them, suppressing the individuality and uniqueness that has grown and developed over the years.

Perhaps one of our tasks, as we grow older, is to re-educate society by moving beyond these cultural stereotypes and refusing to be typecast in this way. I don't mean going round acting like juveniles, for nothing is more embarrassing for all concerned. I mean, rather, claiming the freedom to be more truly ourselves than we have ever before felt the courage or the right to be.

When I was a child, I talked like a child, I thought like a child,
I reasoned like a child. When I became an adult,
I put childish ways behind me.
(1 Corinthians 13:11)

Heavenly Father,
more ancient than time,
younger than the most newborn babe,
proving that age is not only relative
but also a heavenly gift
to be treasured
for all that it brings
to each stage of life,
thank you for all that I have learned
on my journey.
This I have discovered:
that there is a wondrous freedom
in being older.
So many of my former expectations
and burdens of ambition
no longer hold such sway.
I feel released to be more truly me
than I've ever allowed myself before.
Time now is too precious to squander
on living a life designed by others –
an off-the-shelf template
that slots me into a pre-packaged picture
of how they perceive I should be.
Give me the courage to resist
the pressure to fit in for conformity's sake.
I place my hand
firmly in your own.
Lead me along the path
you have prepared
just for me.
Lead me towards
my destiny.

Spirit of Courage and Truth,
give me wings
to soar
beyond myself
and the narrow limits –
born of the fear
of what others
might say –
that I, myself, have set.

Do not allow
me to hide
in the shadows
of the passing years.
Call me out
to walk in the Light
of the Son.

Creator God,
I am *me*.
Created by *you*.
This is who
I truly am.

Retelling your story

Which of us, as children, did not find our level of excitement rise at the magic words, 'Once upon a time . . .'? These words usually ushered in a world of fantastic make-believe that allowed our imaginations to run riot. But we do not have to turn to fiction for amazing stories. We need only to look within. Your story, like that of everyone else, is unique. You may have had similar experiences to others but no one, not even an identical twin, could have lived your life exactly as you have.

We can retell our story in various ways. We may, for example, simply recount it as a straightforward cataloguing of times and events. Or we can make the telling a quest for personal and spiritual meaning; a *retelling* of the past, in the light of our current experience, so that it becomes a vehicle of learning for informing and reshaping the present and the future.

If we are to do the latter, we need to try to reinterpret past events in a way that 'moves them on'. Telling our stories in this way can help free us from constantly repeating negative life-tapes, and can thus heal us from painful or hurtful memories that lock us into the past.

When we try to reinterpret our stories and see old patterns in new ways, we begin a process of reclaiming and owning our past, coming to terms and integrating both the good and the bad from it so that it becomes a springboard into the future.

'For I know the plans
I have for you,'
declares the Lord,
'plans to give you
a hope and a future.'

(Jeremiah 29:11)

Saviour,
as I look back I see
so many memories.
Some are precious inheritances
from the past.
Others are the opposite,
holding me back
and locking me in
to where I no longer want
to be.
When you fed the five thousand
you gathered up all
that was not used,
so that nothing was wasted.
You re-create and make all things
work together for good –
even 12 baskets of leftovers.
I hold up to you
all that I have been,
all that I am.
Help me to retell
and re-create
my story,
to see old patterns
in new ways,
to weave together
the bad with the good.
Reshape my story.
Reshape me.

Jesus,
when you met your disciples
on the Emmaus Road,
they were locked
into despair.
They were unable to recognise you.
Though it was Springtime,
the desolation of winter
filled their minds and hearts.

But you reshaped the story.
You gave them
a new understanding.
Then their hearts were opened
to see all that had happened,
in a totally new way.

Father God,
my past
is what has shaped me.
My present
is where I stand.
My future,
together with my present and past,
lies cradled
in your hand.

Space and time

In the periods of our lives when time is a precious commodity and there seems no room for us to 'do our own thing', the prospect of space and free time can seem like an impossible dream. But then, when the dream is realised, the reality of it can be disconcerting.

Maybe we become so programmed by our so-busy schedules filling our days to the brim that, in a way, we have no need to take responsibility: the days 'happen' to us, rather than us controlling them. Then, when the dreamed-of day *does* arrive, for some the reality is even better than they could have hoped for whilst, for others, deciding how to fill all the space and time that has at last opened up can be a problem of sizeable proportions.

For all of us, however much we have, space and time are precious gifts from God and, like all heavenly gifts, we should treat them with the care and respect they deserve.

Jesus had a hugely demanding schedule, having the whole world to save and only three short years in which to do it, but he seemed always to be mindful about discerning how best the space and time in each day should be used. Sometimes, he appears to have left tasks uncompleted because he needed to go away and pray, or to spend a period just with his disciples, or to attend to something else that he felt deserved prioritising. And sometimes, of course, he spent time simply relaxing and unwinding, either alone or in the company of close friends, like Martha and Mary.

However busy we think we are, like Jesus we need 'down' time; time in which to come face to face with ourselves, stripped of all distracting activity.

The book of Genesis draws a picture of God the Father writing a day off into his script for creating the Universe: surely words of wisdom about balancing the various demands on our space and time.

Jesus said: 'Give Caesar what is his,
and give God what is his.'
(Matthew 22:21b)

God of Wisdom,
'retired' is a disconcerting word
for someone as active as me.
It's resonant with implications
of withdrawing to the sidelines.
But I'm not ready yet for that.
So help me to refocus
and to harmonise my energies,
together with all this new-found spare time,
into ways that are pleasing to you.

Open my eyes to opportunities.
Give me the wisdom
to discern which to take up
and which to lay aside.
Help me not to be
a 'busy-body',
but rather a disciple waiting on you,
willing and eager to seek and to do
your will in all things.

Jesus,
more spare cash, more free time,
more space in my mind than I've ever known before:
these are precious gifts,
pearls beyond price,
with which you have blessed me.
Show me how they may be used
in your service
and to your greater glory.

Loving God,
time is weighing heavily
on my hands
and the space in each day
is pressing in.
I'm face to face with myself
and I'm not sure I like
all that I see.
It felt far better
when the weeks were filled
with distracting activity.

I suspect you have led me
to this moment
and that there are lessons here
you wish me to learn.
So help me to honour this space
and to use this time
as you would have me do.

God of Time,
this is a blessed time for me
and the days don't seem long enough
for all I want to fit in.
I pray for those for whom retirement
has brought only worry and loss.
Show me how I may be
a source of comfort and hope
to those who are not
as fortunate as me.

Speaking your mind

If a survey was conducted about what are the most important and precious aspects of a democratic society, I imagine that freedom of expression would top the poll. However, the pressure to conform can be as alive and well in democratic societies, in its own way, as it is in totalitarian states. Accepted norms can become very pressurising, such that it can take considerable courage to step outside the silence imposed by self, family, social culture or religious norms.

It is significant that the phrase, 'speaking your mind', has a predominantly negative connotation – as if saying what we feel compelled to say is inappropriate social behaviour. And yet that is precisely what this particular phase of life can bring: freedom from the fear of what might be the consequences if we respond to our instincts, our heart's prompting, to speak out on particular issues. As we grow older, we hopefully grow more self-assured. No longer is there the same need to be constrained by concerns about whether expressing strongly held convictions might harm career prospects or people's opinion of us.

Claiming the freedom to speak and act as we feel prompted can be one of the great joys of growing older, potentially leading to an inner liberation from all sorts of things that may hold us captive; inappropriate attitudes, for example, or mental scripts that no longer fit.

Maybe one of the most important roles that the senior members of any society can play is to be prophetic, speaking out of their own life experiences, when they feel compelled, to current situations. If these mature voices are silent, then it is not only a great loss to society but also a denial of God's calling and the example of Jesus. People may not listen, but that knowledge does not exonerate us from playing our part.

Therefore, my friends,
be eager to prophesy.

(1 Corinthians 14:39)

Dear God,
how much easier it is
to go with the flow
of received opinion,
rather than stand out
against the crowd.

It is not easy
to speak my mind,
knowing that it will
set me apart
from the majority.

And yet,
the years would not have given me anything,
if I hold back
from saying what I feel so strongly
in my mind and heart
to be true.

You set us an example in Jesus
when he spoke out
about so many situations
and attitudes
that stopped society
from living out
your creative will.

I am a Christian –
a follower of Christ –
so how can I
do other?

Holy Spirit of God,
there is a wonderful liberation
in being the age I am.
How often,
over the years,
I have struggled against the fear
of what people would think
about me,
if I dared to speak
out of turn
when I felt prompted
by a situation –
or even,
maybe,
prompted
by you?

Now,
the words come easier.
Now my mind is not so enclosed
by fear.
And now I can hear,
so much clearer than before,
your voice in me.

Heavenly Father,
I think about your prophets of old
and where we would be
if they had not spoken out
as they did.
I think of the prophets of today
who are equally important
to our humanity.
Bless them all,
past and present,
for their courage and their witness.
May I be equally brave,
when the situation requires it of me.

Taking time to contemplate

When we are young and life seems full to the brim with getting and doing, building and raising, our prayer life – if we make time for it at all – can be similarly busy. There can seem so many people and situations to pray for and so little time in which to do it that we spend all the time available bombarding God with our petitions. As we grow older, though, our priorities change. That which seemed so desperately important now is seen to be less so, and vice versa.

Hopefully, one of the things age can teach us is that in prayer few, if any, words are necessary; simply bringing ourselves and, therefore, our concerns into God's presence and just 'being' is one of the most profound forms of praying. A person with a 'still' centre, radiating a sense of peace and tranquillity from the core of their being, is a pearl beyond price in our hectic and un-peaceful world.

However, this stillness does not happen by accident. It is the product of regularly making time to withdraw from the many demands and distractions of the everyday in order just to sit in God's presence and 'wait upon the Lord'. The sense of God's love and peace breathed into your soul is the most wondrous of feelings. It nourishes you and strengthens you, in the very depths of your being, in a way that nothing else on earth can.

'I just sits and looks at him on his cross and he just looks back at me,' declared the farm labourer, when asked what he did in the church each evening, on his way home from work in the fields.

Jesus said, 'When you pray, go into your room, close the door
and pray to your Father, who is unseen . . .
And when you pray, do not keep on babbling like pagans,
for they think they will be heard
because of their many words.
Do not be like them, for your Father knows what you need
before you ask him.'
(Matthew 6:6a, 7-8)

Heavenly Father,
even when my life was brimming over
with good things that preoccupied me,
demanding much of my energy
and nearly all of my time,
I felt such a deep hunger in my soul
for the nourishment
only you can give.
And when I found a brief time
in which to pray,
there were so many people
and situations to bring
before you
that it became like a celestial shopping list
of favours.
It was not even pleasing
to me,
so how could it have been pleasing
to you?
It is only now,
with my life slowed down,
that I can truly see
how imbalanced I had become.
Forgive me.
From now on,
I want it to be different.
From now on,
I shall sit at your feet.
And wait on you.
And listen.
In silence.
And peace.
How good it all sounds.
How good it all feels.
It is as if
I have at last
come home
to you.

Lord,
may I be a person
with a centre that is still.

A place where
you and I meet
and truly communicate,
without my words
getting in the way.

A place where
I discover truths
about myself
that I did not have ears
to hear before.

A place where I draw
from the wellspring
of your wisdom
and your strength
and your love.

A place where
true healing
of spirit
takes place.

A place of
Wonder
and
Joy
and
Peace.

Spirit of God,
it was not in the storm,
nor in the tempest,
that Elijah heard you –
but in the whispering breeze
that followed.

Vibrantly alive

Some of the most vibrantly alive people I have ever known, have been those in their 80s, 90s or even 100s. These were people who were comfortable with being old, who welcomed each new day as a precious gift and who could still, despite all the inevitable diminishments that such an age brings, view life as an ongoing miracle to be lived fully and richly.

Old people such as these can be a fixed point, an oasis of calm and stability in a fast-changing, unpredictable world. They have lived through all the vicissitudes a long life inevitably brings and afford living proof that the human spirit can come through victorious in the face of whatever life chooses to present it with. Such people can also be proof of the value of just 'being', as opposed to 'doing'.

Of course, they don't just suddenly 'end up', in this way. It is the product of an attitude to life developed over a period of many years and lived out in the everyday. If we aspire to being such old people, in our turn, we need to start living in such a way at as early an age as possible.

What more precious thing can we gift to society than being places of calm: peace-filled people in the midst of our turbulent world?

God said:
'I've been carrying you on my back
from the day you were born.
And I'll keep on carrying you when you're old.
I'll be there, bearing you when you're old and grey.
I've done it and will keep on doing it,
carrying you on my back,
saving you.'
(Isaiah 46:3b-4)

Do not forget me,
Lord,
now my active days
are past,
and I can no longer
serve you,
as I used to do.

Still remember me.

Remember me,
heavenly Father,
as the evening shades
draw in
and my busy world
of yesteryear
narrows to an easy chair.

Do not forget me.

'*Forget* you?
I will not forget you!
See,
I have engraved you
on the palms
of my hands.'

(The reference is to Isaiah 49:15b-16a)

Jesus,
is the world really
more turbulent
than in my young day,
or is it just the speed
with which news spreads
that makes it seem that way?

I pray for all those
for whom this world is a hard
or lonely place.

Help me to be
an oasis of calm,
a stable point,
for all in need.

A place where love
and peace
and hope
and time to listen
may be found.

Generous God,
thank you
for the precious gift
of each new day.
Help me to value
and to use
every single golden moment
you give me
in the way
that most pleases you
and to your greater glory.

Wisdom people

'That night God appeared to Solomon and said to him, "Ask for whatever you want me to give you." "Give me wisdom and knowledge, that I may lead this people," Solomon answered' (2 Chronicles 1:7, 10a; *NIV*). Solomon could have chosen great wealth or great power. Instead, he chose wisdom – and proved, thereby, what a wise man he already was.

A curious mind, always ready and willing to learn new things, always thirsty for knowledge, clearly has a profound effect on the physical. Research has shown the intimate link between a lively, enquiring mind and physical well-being. One of the most entrancing things about children is their wonder and delight in everything they encounter. Life, for children, is one long learning curve. Somewhere along the way through adulthood, however, with all its expectations and preoccupations, we can all too easily lose this natural joy in learning.

As life becomes less demanding, opportunities present themselves to redevelop that sense of curiosity, wonder and excitement in learning for its own sake. The phrase 'keeping the grey cells active' is particularly relevant.

It is one of those occasions where 'grey' as a description is good!

If you turn your ear to wisdom
and apply your heart to understanding,
and if you call out for insight
and cry aloud for understanding,
and if you look for it as for silver
and search for it as for hidden treasure,
then you will understand the fear of the Lord
and find the knowledge of God.

(Proverbs 2:2-5)

God of Wisdom,
words of human wisdom
can be very persuasive,
but they awake in their listeners
a purely human response.

There is a different plane,
a different reality.
When our human wisdom
reaches its limit,
it is then, Lord,
that your power takes over.
It is then that the true conversion
of mind and heart
is brought to fruition.

So, guide my thinking
with your wisdom and discernment.
May I have clear-eyed vision
for the decisions I have to make.

When I have concluded
what I think is right,
may my conclusions be tested
and purified
in the furnace of your wisdom.

Then fill me with your courage
and a steady sense of purpose,
and walk with me
the way you and I have chosen.

Jesus,
there is such a contrast
between the wisdom of the world
and the foolishness
of the message
of your cross.
I kneel before you
full of human ignorance,
but so longing to learn
your truth.

Help me to understand
better and deeper.
May I touch the hem
of your garment,
the threads of which
are woven with the wisdom
and knowledge
of heaven.

Dear God,
you said to Paul –
and so to us all –
'When you are weak,
then I am strong.'
I know it
and I believe it,
in the very core of my being;
any ignorance of mine
is no impediment
to the fulfilment of your will.
For,
what I have not,
you will give
of your own.
All I have to do,
is open myself up
to you.

(The reference is to 2 Corinthians 12:7-10)

End-piece 1: *The* lifeline

When [Peter] saw the wind
he was afraid and,
beginning to sink,
cried out,
'Lord, save me!'
Immediately,
Jesus reached out his hand
and caught him.

(Matthew 14:30-31a)

Jesus,
you are my lifeline.
When the winds and waves
of this world
are overwhelming me
and I cry out in fear,
you are always there.

You are my lifeline.
'Take courage!'
you say.
'It is I.
Do not be afraid.'

You are my lifeline.
Just as much needed
when the water is calm
and when I vainly think
it is I who is in control.

You are my lifeline.
Reach out your hand.
Take mine.
May I be a person of great faith
in your eternal presence.

End-piece 2: The gates of heaven

Just beyond our ordinary everyday vision there are untold wonders that God wishes to share with each one of us; not once in a lifetime, but day by day and minute by minute.

The gates of heaven do not just lie in some wondrous, other-world place before which, one day, we hope to stand. They are, in fact, to be found also within our hearts, where we can meet God in our everyday lives. If we wish them to swing wide open, all we have to do is to give over our hearts and lives into God's care and service.

'Be eager to do right,
and change your hearts and lives.
Here I am!
I stand at the door and knock.
If you hear my voice and open the door,
I will come in and eat with you,
and you will eat with me.'

After the vision of these things
I looked,
and there before me
was an open door in heaven.
(Revelation 3:19b, 4:1a; *Youth Bible*)